Rose Care:

Home Gardening Tips For Beginners

By Michael Edwards

Table Of Contents

Table Of Contents	1

Meaning and history behind roses	3

How to select healthy roses and where to buy them	6

The Anatomy of Roots, Stems and Leaves of Roses	9

Potted Roses vs Bare Root Roses	11

Differences between shrub roses, climbing roses, and groundcover roses	17

Heirloom Roses vs Grafted roses	20

Knockout Roses	22

Standard care for roses	25

How and when to prune roses	28

Tips for decorating and landscaping with roses 31

How to plant and pot your roses	34

Differentiating healthy root roses versus dead roots on roses	38

How to care for cut roses	43

Importance of humidity and air movement in preventing diseases	46
How to get your rose bloom more	49
How to Transplant Roses	51
Caring for Roses in Different Seasons	53
Common pest and diseases	57
How to get rid of Japanese beetles	61
Special Thanks	65

Meaning and history behind roses

It's almost universally understood that red roses mean love and romance. They are the traditional Valentine's Day gift between lovers and will pack every florist's shop from February 1 until after the holiday.

The meanings and symbolism behind red roses, however, are deep-rooted and ancient. For centuries of human history, the red petals of the rose have sparked relationships and spoken passion and desire.

Red itself is a profound color of emotion. In the West, it is a color that signifies both danger and love, two things that aren't always separate. Both the Greeks and the Romans gave special significance to the red rose particularly, tying it in with their goddesses of love. During banquets commemorating goddesses like Aphrodite and Venus, red roses would festoon the temples and the petals of flowers would cover the floors. Rose petals would also be put into the drinks and were thought to be aphrodisiacs for the occasion of lovers.

During Roman times, it became common for peasants to raise roses to give as tribute to their rulers, especially the emperor. Later, roses were often used to pay debts to sovereigns due to their association with wealth and power. The common hobby garden of roses didn't leave the rich's purview until the 19th century.

The tradition of giving flowers as gifts between friends and lovers, however, didn't really come about until the Middle Ages, when lovers began to give them as tokens of affection. A Swedish King popularized the idea of sending flowers when he used them to send messages in the 1700s, copying from the Persian use of flowers as messenger's tools to keep the enemy from understanding the true message. For the Swede, obviously, the reasons were less tactical.

Today, the mixture of the Swedish tradition, the Roman and Greek meanings, and the modern proclivity for things of beauty have all come together. The ultimate expression of these is through the gift of red roses for Valentine's Day (or any other day) to tell a lover your feelings towards them.

In fact, roses have gone beyond this with colors

tilting the rainbow and signifying all types of meaning to those who send and receive them. There are over 100 species of rose and the name itself comes from the Latin 'rosa.'

Whatever your occasion or whatever the reason, giving a single or a full bouquet of roses is the best way to signify meaning and devotion to your chosen one.

How to select healthy roses and where to buy them

Selecting Rose Plants

Picking out a rose plant may sound easy, but gardeners are often faced with many options such as bare-root, containerized, grafted, own-root, and various grades. All of these options may play a part in the decision-making process of selecting roses for the garden. Of prime importance is selecting varieties that will fit into a garden based upon size of the garden, local growing conditions, and varieties that the grower likes and feels will fit into his plan.

Where To Buy Roses

Rose plants can be purchased locally through garden centers and other retail outlets or by mail. Keep in mind that local outlets can offer the gardener flexibility but may not have a wide selection; mail order tends to offer a wide selection but the flexibility as to when plants need to be purchased is limited. Plants bought locally are sold either bare-root or potted. Mail order plants are almost always sold bare-root. Which is better? When ordered or bought from a reputable dealer, both are good, and it's just a matter of preference. Many older roses are only available bare root through specialty mail order nurseries.

Bare-root roses are dormant plants that are sold to the gardener with no soil around the roots; instead, they have moist packing material such as peat or wood shavings around the roots. Bare-root plants are sold in garden centers as "packaged" plants. Packaged as well as mail order roses may also have their canes covered with wax. This helps prevent drying while in storage or in the retail store. The wax doesn't need to be removed. It will eventually degrade and break away from the canes.

Canes on bare-root plants should be plump and green with smooth, unshriveled bark. They should also feel heavy. A dried-out plant will feel light, and the twigs will be brittle. Bare-root plants should be ordered with instructions to ship them when planting is suitable for your area. If bare-root packaged roses are bought locally, try to select them as soon as possible after the shipment is received at the store. Stores generally hold packaged plants in warm areas that cause them to break dormancy, producing premature, weak growth that can devitalize the plant. If bare-root roses can't be planted immediately, they may be held up to two weeks in an area that is cool (40°F). Keep the canes and roots moist during this time by covering them with moist material such as peat moss or wood shavings.

Heeling rose plants to hold them prior to planting

If plants need to be held longer than 2 weeks, it is a good idea to heel them in outdoors. This is done by laying the plants in a shallow trench and covering the roots with soil. The canes may also be covered if drying is a concern.

The Anatomy of Roots, Stems and Leaves of Roses

Canes - Canes are the main branches of the rose bush, emerging from the root mass in the caseof an 'own root' bush and emerging from the bud union on a grafted rose.

Shank - The main stem of the rootstock rose. The 'preferred' roses has been grafted onto the top of the shank.

Bud Union - the area between the roots and the stems where the bud of the desired variety was grafted onto the rootstock.

Roots - There are two types of roots.
• The 'anchor' roots are thick and strong, they hold the rose bush upright while it is growing. They also store nutrients during the winter season.

• The 'hair roots' are the feeder roots. Their main job is to absorb the nutrients in the soil as they become available.

Basal Breaks - Basal breaks are new canes sprouting from the bud union (the graft) on a grafted rose. These new canes are the way the rose renews itself. Sometimes mistaken for the 'sucker' cane which does not emerge from the bud union.

Leaf - The leaves of roses are pinnately compound -that means they are made up of leaflets arranged along the side of a common axis with one leaflet on the end. The example is of a five-leaflet leaf. Roses also have 3-leaflet leaves and many have 7-leaflets or more.

Petiole - The tiny stem holding all the leaflets.
Petiolul - a subdivision of the petiole that connects a leaflet to the petiole.

Leaf Margin - The edge of the leaflet, usually "toothed" like a saw blade. Some roses have very smooth leaf margins, others are very deeply 'dentate' or toothed.

Stipule - The tissue at the point of attachment of petiole to stem. Often long and exaggerated.

Auricle - the 'ear-like' projection from the tip of the stipule.

Potted Roses vs Bare Root Roses

Potted rose

Garden centers can offer both containerized and potted roses. Containerized plants are bought as bare-root plants by the nurserymen, placed in containers, and sold as growing plants that same season. The root development may not be very extensive with these plants and so extra care may be needed when transplanting to the garden. Some potted plants may have been grown at the nursery for a longer time resulting in a very extensive root system. The extensive root system holds the soil ball together resulting in an easier job of transplanting without the problem of the soil ball falling apart. Due to economics, one is not likely to find many of these plants for sale unless they were overwintered from the previous season. Containerized plants can be planted any time during the growing season with spring or early season planting preferred for northern growing areas. Fall planting of roses can be done, but may need extra winter protection and the earlier plants are planted, the better. Bare-root roses can be shipped and planted only in the spring while they are dormant.

Bareroot roses

They are only viable when the plant is still in its dormant phase. If a bareroot becomes heated in-store or during transport, it may take it from its dormant state and produce weak growth. Therefore, they need to be planted as quickly as possible, keeping them moist at all times before planting. When purchasing, select a vigorous rose specimen that has a well-developed, fibrous root systems with smooth green stems that have a diameter of 7-8mm.

Differences between bareroot and potted roses

Bare-root roses lack beauty when you buy them but produce gorgeous blooms just the same.
Many gardeners find they've actually got more versatility with bare-root roses. Sure, they look like they're practically dead – just a worrisome mass of sticks and roots – but the fact is you'll likely have a wider variety of roses to choose from than container-grown selections.
You can sometimes find bare-root roses at garden centers early in the spring, but you'll be limited to

the few dozen varieties in stock. They're typically packed into plastic bags or cardboard boxes with their stems sticking out. (Be careful of these roses sold later in the season when they're temptingly marked down. They're cut-rate for a reason. And if a bare-root rose has well-developed leaves on it, don't buy it! It's getting too far along in its growth and will have trouble getting established once you plant it.)

Most often, gardeners purchase bare-root roses by mail. (They're much easier to ship than container roses, and the selection is practically limitless). When they arrive, the roots will be packed in sawdust, a straw-like material or very loose soil or mulch – all of which is then wrapped in plastic to keep the roots moist. The top part will look like fat sticks, several inches to a foot or so long. They may show almost no sign of life other than some red bud-like growths that will turn eventually into stems.

One of the great things about bare-root roses is they can be planted earlier in the growing season since there are no leaves to get nipped by frost. However, they can't be planted too early or the rosebushes will languish in the cold, wet soil. That said, be careful not too sink them in the ground too late in the season either, or they won't take off.

As a rule, bare-root roses can be planted as early as six weeks before your region's last average frost date in spring and no later than two weeks after that date. The last average frost date is roughly in March for the southern third of the country, April for middle of the US and May for the northern regions. If you're not sure about timing for your area, check with your local Cooperative Extension Service, a knowledgeable gardening neighbor or your local garden center professional for regional specifics.

As long as you plant your bare-root roses at the right time, they're likely to take off faster and better than their containerized counterparts. That's because these wonderful plants can focus their energies on good root development instead of working to support extensive leaf growth during the stressful time of planting.

Unlike bare-root roses, container-grown roses usually have good looks on their side. These plants are typically sold in 1-gallon sizes or larger. You'll find them in springtime at all kinds of garden centers, and they're usually nicely leafed out and may even have flowers on them. Beautiful as those flowers are – and as nice as it is to have a live visual of what they look and smell like – the blooms are actually a bad thing because the bush's energy naturally goes toward sustaining the flowers instead of focusing on root development. If you can't help yourself and just have to buy that blooming plant, steel yourself and trim the flowers off before planting the bush in your garden. (You can always

put the flowers in a vase to enjoy indoors.)
When buying container roses, look for plants with well-developed root systems. The roots shouldn't be bursting out of the pot, but they shouldn't be practically nonexistent either. To find out what lies beneath the soil, grasp the rose's main stem and give it a gentle wiggle. If it pulls right out of the pot with just a few or weak roots, pack it back in and don't buy it. A rose without a good root system isn't likely to thrive. It'll probably struggle through the summer and die out over winter.

One of the advantages of buying container-grown roses is that they're easier to keep healthy if it's going to be a while before you can plant them. Just be sure to keep your plants well-watered and in a sunny (but not baked) spot.

Another good thing is that container roses can be planted later in the growing season – anytime after the danger of frost has passed. (Just avoid planting them in very hot weather when daytime temperatures exceed 90 degrees F.) In fact, you can add container roses to your garden into fall – but no later than six weeks before your region's frost date. They need some time to get established before extremely cold weather hits. (Six weeks before the first frost date is roughly September for the northern regions, October for middle sections and November for southern areas of the country. But again, consult an expert who lives in your area to be sure.)

No matter which type of rose you choose – bareroot or container-grown – just be sure to give your plant a good start. If given proper care, your rosebush will thank you with years of gorgeous blooms!

Differences between shrub roses, climbing roses, and groundcover roses

Roses (Rosa spp.) are a popular flowering shrub planted in home gardens. Roses are grouped into three classifications: bush, climbing and shrub. All of these rose forms appear in both modern and old garden roses. Modern roses are those plants bred since 1867 when the first hybrid tea rose was introduced. Old garden roses are the ones around before that historic date, which include wild roses. The differences between rose varieties include plant size, flower fragrance and the amount of blossoms.

Size

Rose varieties are available in many different sizes. Climbing roses are the largest of the roses because the stems act like vines and climb upward on supports. Standard rose bush varieties are usually

36 inches tall, while patio rose bushes are between 18 to 24 inches high. Groundcover roses produce low mounds 24 to 30 inches tall spreading up to 8 feet wide. Polyanthus rose varieties grow less than 24 inches high. The smallest of the rose varieties is the miniature rose, which reaches less than 12 inches tall.

Blooming Time

Rose breeders have hybridized roses throughout the centuries attempting to extend their flowering season. Modern roses are nearly ever-blooming, like the hybrid musk shrub rose. Grandifloras, floribundas and polyanthas produce a large number of blooms from spring until fall. Most old-fashioned varieties bloom only once a year. These old garden roses include damask roses (Rosa damascena) and centifolia roses (Rosa centifolia), with both types blooming in the spring.

Fragrance

The types of rose scents (more than 24 in all) vary widely, including rose, orris, violet, apple, lemon, raspberry and wine. Many varieties of roses have a fragrance, but some do not. Nearly all old-fashioned rose varieties have fragrance. "Double Delight" hybrid tea rose (Rosa "Double Delight") produces a sweet spicy scent in U.S. Department of Agriculture plant hardiness zones 5 through 9.

Not many floribunda varieties produce a strong scent, but "Honey Perfume" floribunda rose (Rosa "Honey Perfume") gives off a strong spicy honey-like fragrance in USDA zones 6 through 10. "Sun Sprinkles" miniature rose (Rosa "Sun Sprinkles") grows well in USDA zones 6 through 10 and gives off a spicy musky scent.

Cut Flowers
Many varieties of roses produce groups or sprays of blossoms, which do not make the best cut flowers. For cut flowers, look for varieties with just a single bloom on top of a long stem, which are commonly found among the hybrid tea roses. This rose variety produces conical-shaped blossoms, which look like the classic romantic rose. One rose variety suitable for cut flowers is the "Double Delight" hybrid tea rose (Rosa "Double Delight"), which grows best in USDA zones 6 through 10. This hybrid rose variety produces cream-colored blossoms with red petal tips, which appear from early spring throughout summer.

Heirloom Roses vs Grafted roses

Growers initially began producing Heirloom-roses as a response to the prevalence of Rose Mosaic Virus within the industry. This nasty virus was spread through grafting. Growers found that they could greatly reduce the spread of RMV if they used virus-free stock plants. Soon the industry discovered that roses grown on their own natural roots (and not those of another variety) had other advantages too:

- Heirloom roses are hardier than grafted roses because their crown has not been weakened. The bud union of a grafted rose is vulnerable to cold and can be easily damaged during a hard winter.

- Heirloom roses come back true to variety if frozen to the ground, because they have their own root system. Winter kill is less likely.

- Heirloom roses are shaplier because they

send up shoots from their Heirloom. This creates a fuller plant over time, which adds to increased vigor, bloom, and life expectancy.

- Heirloom roses have no rootstock suckers, meaning more energy is sent to the main plant.

For hundreds of years, home gardeners have been propagating their own roses by taking cuttings and growing them on their own roots. With Heirloom Roses, gardeners can enjoy the many benefits own-root roses have to offer without having to worry about rootstock.

Knockout Roses

Knockout Roses - The Rose for Beginners

Called by a variety of names, "Knockouts", "Knockouts Roses", "Knock Out Roses", "Rose Knockouts", the plant is designed for the beginner rosarian. Growing roses for some people presents a task greater than they want to get involved with. Quite honestly, growing roses is not as difficult as some would lead you to believe. Nevertheless, a rose plant has been bred that eliminates many of the growing difficulties perceived.

What makes the Knockout Rose a good rose for beginners is its characteristics:
- It is easy to grow
- Disease Resistant
- Requires little pruning
- Blooms the first year
- Cold Hardy
- Heat Tolerant
- Long Blooming - blooms up to 7 months
- Grows in full sun or partial shade

- Re-blooming
- Fast Growing
- Pest Resistant

The Knockout is considered by many to be a landscape plant, that is, to be used as hedges and such. They are very well suited as hedges because they blossom for such a long time and require no deadheading. Deadheading is the process of removing the dead flowers in order to spur on growth of new flowers. In a landscape plant like the Knockout Rose, if you had to deadhead 40-50 feet of bushes you could be in for quite a task on a routine basis. So, "no deadheading needed" is a strong plus for the Knockout.

Disease resistance is also a strong plus for the Knockout, which is highly resistant to blackspot disease. Blackspot disease is a fungus that grows on the leaves, and is normally the result of the leaf being damp at night. At its worst blackspot can completely defoliate a bush. So again, being resistant to blackspot is a great plus.

If any rose could be called "no maintenance" the Knockout Rose would be the one, although "low maintenance" would be better terminology.
When first introduced, the plant was greeted with great excitement and have quickly spread throughout the country and appear in many landscape plans. The bushes are available in a

number of colors including red, pink, white and yellow. By itself the Knockout Rose is a hit among gardeners, but no sooner was the Knockout being planted, then here comes the Double Knockout Rose.

The "Double" describes the fact that the Double Knockout Rose has double the petals on the blossom, giving them a richer, fuller look. The colors, varieties, and richness of the Knockout Roses and Double Knockout Roses can only be fully appreciated by seeing them in bloom.

Standard care for roses

Rose Tree Garden

A rose tree garden is a sight to behold! From the palest pinks to the deepest reds, from tight buds to full blooms and everything else in between, you combine the best of both worlds - the beauty of roses with the boon of space. Indeed, if you do not have the space to cultivate roses, then a tree rose garden is the next best thing. Here are tips to get you started on the right and easy path.

Purchase from a Reputable Nursery

Why worry about things like grafting when you can purchase rose trees in all their glory? Just make sure that you purchase the stocks for your rose tree garden from a reputable nursery as you want the rose tree to survive even under the care of a novice.

To make your gardening life easier, opt for a rose tree that requires little to no deadheading. Varieties like Double Knockout, Knockout and Carpet are ideal for this purpose although you can always ask the nursery staff for their recommendations.

Prepare the Soil Beforehand

Before proceeding to the nursery to purchase your initial stocks, you have to prepare the beds on which the rose trees will be transplanted. You have to ensure that the beds are just in the right condition plenty of compost mixed into the soil and good drainage, to name a few. To start your rose tree garden, you must first soak the rose standards in a bucketful of water while you dig the hole. This will ensure that the roots absorb plenty of water before transplantation. (The secret to transplanting roses is hyper-watering, by the way)

Plant the Rose Trees the Right Way

Of course, you just do not dig a hole in the ground and stick your rose tree in! You might as well get a shovel and whack at it for a few minutes until the two grafts are mangled beyond description.

Besides, you must design the garden to achieve the best effect. Thus, knowing exactly where to plant will make your rose tree garden more impressive, more expressive and more attractive! In short, you do not end up with a jungle of roses. Here are the basic steps to planting nursery-bought rose trees:

Dig an 18-inch deep hole with a width of 2 feet and then loosen the soil for another 6-12 inches. Into this loosened soil, mix in compost. Do the same with the soil from the dug hole but set it aside for the meantime.

Place your rose tree into the hole making sure that its roots are spread adequately and the bud junction will stand 1 inch under the soil once it is covered.

Cover the plant and its roots with the compost-soil mix.

Place a sturdy stake to support the trunk of the tree rose. Be sure to tie the trunk to the stake with an elastic bind.

Add the root starter and rose fertilizer to the whole set-up.

You have to repeat these steps to all the rose trees. And voila! You now have a rose tree garden. Now, sit back, relax and let Nature perform most of the work.

How and when to prune roses

Pruning your rose bushes is good for the bushes. While it will take you some time to master the art of pruning your roses, it is quite difficult to kill roses with bad or poor pruning. So, it is better that you make an effort to prune your roses rather than letting them grow wild.

If you prune your rose bushes, you will encourage growth of new blooms and branches, it will aid in the removal of dead branches, enhance air circulation and improve the shape of the bushes.

Make sure you invest in proper pruning equipment like long gloves, loppers with long handles and by-pass pruning shears. Keep the equipment clean and sharp. Always make sure that you start pruning the bush from the base and then work your way upwards. Make all the cuts at an angle of 45 degrees and the cuts should be clean and around quarter inch above the buds. Cut out any branches that look dead, dried or broken. If you notice cane borers on your branches, use a white glue to seal off the holes in the branches. A good glue to use is Elmer's. Make sure you open up the center of the bush to facilitate air circulation and allow the plant to receive more sunlight.

Usually rose bushes should be pruned in spring. Look for forsythia blooming in your area to begin pruning your roses. In case you do not see forsythia around you, the look at the leaf buds. You should begin pruning when the leaf buds swell up and attain a reddish color.

The fre◻uency of pruning

Never prune very often. This type of roses should be pruned no more, no less than every three years. If you want to trim your plant for aesthetic reasons, this can be done anytime you want it.

The ideal time to prune

The ideal time in pruning roses is during spring when growth is just starting. Removing old, dead wood from the center of your rose plant will surely stimulate growth. This in turn will also facilitate added air circulation and safeguard your rose plant from attack from diseases. If you wish to prune your plant during the summer because you merely just want to retain the shape of your rose plant, you can do this.

Clean pruning tools

As a general rule, use pruning shears to prune roses. Always make sure that they are clean before you use them. Rubbing alcohol can be a good disinfectant tool or agent for this. Cleaning your pruning shears will significantly reduce the risk of inviting disease to your rose plant.

The right position and angle

Ideally, the branch should be cut at an angle of 45 degrees. This is done to reduce old stumps and to invite added growth. You should also make your cut a quarter of an inch above an outward facing bud in order to achieve an upward and outward growth for your rose plant.

The aforementioned tips are just some of the things you need to put into mind when pruning knockout roses. As mentioned earlier, these roses do not really need an abundance of care and maintenance. All that's needed is for you to know how to plant and to understand the basic fundamentals of watering and pruning and you will do just fine. Pruning these roses will then be a no-brainer!

Tips for decorating and landscaping with roses

Tips For Designing Your Rose Garden

I think the use of landscape roses makes the exterior of any house more graceful, fragrant and inviting. If you select the right varieties to accent and compliment the home's style and your vision, landscape roses will contribute to the success of your landscape and rose garden design.

Finding the perfect roses for your rose garden is not that hard because of the many varieties of roses. The problem lies in choosing the right rose bushes for your landscape needs and the design you are trying to archive.

Roses come in a number of different classes. Each class holds characteristics that make them a great choice for use as landscape ornamentals. As an example, suppose you'd like to have roses growing up and over an archway or trellis or archway or cascading from window boxes. Then the tall growing tea roses are a perfect choice. Tea roses are famous for their wild growing blooms. Use the tea rose and every time you or your guests walk under the archway you'll enjoy a beautiful display of roses.

If a trellis isn't available and you're looking to accent a wall, then why not try a true climbing rose. The beauty of a true climbing rose allows you train the plant into many different looks and effects. I've always loved the way it can be trained to grow so many different ways.
I also love the Floribunda rose when I'm looking for a vibrant splash of background color. When I use the Floribunda rose varieties, I know my garden will be alive with color because of their large and breathtaking sprays of blooms.

I also use the versatile rose as a ground cover or planted in front of other plants to give color and accent. I've also used them as stand alone specimens and trained them into a small tree or as hedges. I think the Rugosa roses are a good choice for this. The goal or impact of the rose is not the varieties or ways it can be grown but the colors they offer in making your garden come alive with a palette of colors.

What I and most gardeners want are healthy rose plants that deliver impact in many sizes, styles, textures, colors and shapes. When considering your design for your rose garden try to choose complimentary colors for your surrounding landscape.

Consider that a simple arrangement of pink roses can deliver the perfect compliment to a stone or marble entranceway or drive. White tea roses can offer a striking contrast against a dark red brick home. Since roses come in so many different colors it is relatively easy to find colors to compliment and enhance any decorating or landscape design you can imagine. Designing your rose garden should be exciting and challenging to say the least. So incorporate your own color favorites and mix styles and textures for an interesting appeal.

Although roses can do well in a variety of temperature zones and climates, make sure you choose the varieties suitable to the area in which you live. This translates into fewer maintenance issues, less pesticides and disease issues promoting overall a healthier rose garden.

How to plant and pot your roses

How to Plant Your Roses

Taking good care of a rose goes beyond how much fertilizer is to be used or how deep the hole should be or if you plan to add fertilizer now or later on. Either way, you must not forget that the most important part in planting a rose is choosing the correct location where to let it grow. There are many things to be considered in choosing a plant's location and this must be dealt with high importance.

Will your chosen location get enough sunlight for the roses? Majority of rose species must receive at least six hours of direct, unfiltered sunlight throughout the day. Even those shade tolerant species must be given about four to six hours of sunlight to do well.

Is the soil healthy? Roses require nutritious soil aside from sunlight in order to survive. The soil must be rich enough to contain all the necessary nutrients the roses need from it. It should not have too much clay or sand. To test out whether it has too much clay or sand, clump it with your hand. If the soil has too much clay, it will hold the mold but will not crumble very easily. If it does crumble easily and does not hold the mold, then it has too much sand. A characteristic of good soil is that it should hold the mold in your hand but would crumble easily. The soil must not be too acidic, nor should it contain much limestone or much chalk.

Last but not the least is to see whether you're going to plant your roses too close to tress or to other plants. There are many trees and plants that pull water for them way beyond their drip line. If you start seeing a lot of roots while digging for a space for your roses, this should be an indication that this would probably create problems sooner or later. There are some climbing rose and some shrubs that are an exception but most rose plants only like to be mixed with other roses or other non-invasive plants.

After you have decided on where to place your rose plant, you can think about how deep the hole should actually be. The hole must be slightly larger than the pot where the plant is. This way, you would encourage the roots of the roses to dig deeper for more water. The depth of the hole, however, is dependent upon your location.

Climate has great effect on your roses, as you should know by now. The colder areas need their plants to be deeper into the soil. It would be a great idea to go around asking people from your area about how deep their plants are. A good piece of advice would be to visit the local gardener's club or a gardening shop near you. Most of the time, people there gather to exchange ideas and or have tips for growing healthier plants. You might even spot a fellow rose-grower whom you could ask. The depth varies according to people but do remember to add fertilizer at the bottom or some bone meal for a good source of phosphorous that would encourage healthy root growth.

Gently spread the roots out slightly and fill-up the hole with soil. You could water the roots before adding more soil to it. Finally, add the refill the last of the soil back into the hole, give it a slight pat to make sure that soil is intact, and you could finally water it again

Bare Root Plants

Soak the roots of the bush for 12-24 hours to help it with the transition back to being in the soil. Prune the roots back one-half inch to encourage new root growth. Dig a hole for your rose bush that is at least two feet in diameter. Mix some compost in with the dirt that you dug out of the hole. Create a mound of dirt in the bottom of the hole and spread the roots over it. Gently pack the remaining soil around the roots making sure that the graft union is slightly below the final soil level. This can be easily checked by placing a straightedge across the hole.

Potted Plants

Potted rose planting is generally the same except all you need to do is pop the plant out of the container and ensure that it is planted at the same depth as it was in the pot.

Your newly planted roses should be mulched, but keep the mulch a few inches away from the stem. They should also be watered daily for the first week and every couple of days after that, adjusting for rainfall.

Once your roses start growing they should be fertilized with a rose specific fertilizer every three months.

The roses should be pruned in early spring before new growth occurs in March. The link below has a good description of the pruning process.

Following these instructions should ensure enjoyment of your roses for many years to come.

Differentiating healthy root roses versus dead roots on roses

How to Tell a Rose Bush is Dead

Roses rest over the winter -- even in mild winters -- to build strength for their lush growth in spring, summer and into fall in warm climates. During the dormant period, roses lose their blooms and leaves. Cold temperatures cause tender growth to darken and die back. However, don't give a rose up for dead because canes are leafless, black and dead-looking as other roses emerge from dormancy; take the time to thoroughly assess its condition before declaring your rose a goner.

Pruning in late winter removes dead growth for a healthier rose.

Roses rest over the winter -- even in mild winters --

to build strength for their lush growth in spring, summer and into fall in warm climates. During the dormant period, roses lose their blooms and leaves. Cold temperatures cause tender growth to darken and die back. However, don't give a rose up for dead because canes are leafless, black and dead-looking as other roses emerge from dormancy; take the time to thoroughly assess its condition before declaring your rose a goner.

- Examine canes for swelling buds in late winter from tip to base. Buds may just look like tiny raised reddish nubs as they emerge from the stem.

- Look for green or deep red stems at the base of the plant. Cold-damaged canes that are black at the tip may still be green and living near the base. The delineation between living and dead tissue is usually apparent, at least on young canes. Older stems may be brownish-gray with a thin, barklike skin.

- Scratch at the skin of a cane with your fingernail looking for green tissue just beneath the surface. This is the plant's cambium layer, which produces new cells. If there is no green, the cane is dead.

- Clean bypass pruners with household

antiseptic cleaner at full strength. The cleaner is as effective at eliminating any lingering plant fungi or disease from the tools as rubbing alcohol or bleach -- often recommended for the purpose -- but is less corrosive to metal tools.

- Put on leather gloves.

- Prune back all canes with dead areas back to green wood, if any, and cut out congested canes in the center of the plant in late winter.

- Clean the blades between each cut when dealing with canes you think may be diseased.

- Check the plant for signs of buds and new shoots in a week or two, Older rose bushes, or the oldest canes on a rose bush, can take longer to bud than younger stems.

- Dig lightly at the base of a plant before removing it and check the plant's roots. Firm, light-colored roots are healthy.

Tip
Sudden wilting of a rose bush during the growing season can be caused by herbicide drifting over from another plant, a root disturbance from a

burrowing animal or girdling of a stem -- when an animal gnaws the cambium layer in a circle around the base of a stem. Quick pruning and replanting, depending on the problem, can save the bush.

Examining bare root roses

Roses are such a popular plant in the home garden, with their beautiful blooms and fragrance, but do you know what to look for when buying bare root roses to plant in the garden?

Gardeners will happily buy bare-root roses to take pride of place in their garden. They painstakingly prepare the soil, plant and water their newly purchased bareroot roses and are then aghast when nothing happens at the start of the growing season. Not one leaf bud shoots out from the branches. They usually put it down to their lack of skill in the gardening department but more often than not, they have bought a bareroot rose bush whose roots have dried out and created a dead rose bush. So they have basically planted a rose bush that was dead to start with.

Of course bare rooted roses do look a little dead when you purchase them. There are no leaves on the plant, just bark, so it is hard for the untrained eye to determine if it's alive or dead. Usually the bare-roots are packaged in some kind of moist media like saw dust which is then held in place by some paper, then wrapped in a plastic bag that is sealed below the bud union. This conceals them so it's impossible to really check out the roots when the rose is packaged this way.

So the only visual detail you can rely on is the bark of the stem itself. What you need to look for is bark that feels soft to the touch and is greenish in color. If the bark is brown, hard and has fine lines along the stems then it's more than likely wood that is dead or dying.
Visible fine lines formed along the stems are caused from the bark shrinking around the stem through lack of moisture. This could be caused by the fibrous roots drying out because there was not enough moisture in the media they were packaged in; not very many fibrous roots were left on the rose bush to begin with, so it couldn't uptake the moisture in the media it was packed in; or poor storage practice of the store where you purchased your rose bush – for example if the roses were left out in the sun and the packaging dried out.

No matter the cause, if the stems look dried out because the bark has shrunk on the stem; the color of the bark is more a woody brown than green and the stem feels hard and looks wrinkly rather than being soft and yielding, don't buy the rose plant. If you look at enough of them, you will get your eyes trained, and be able to differentiate between the healthy looking stems and the dead or dying "sticks" of bare root roses.

How to care for cut roses

One the arts of reviving wilted roses is to prevent this from happening and this comes with prolonging their life for as long as possible after cutting.

Care of cut roses

Roses should always be cut with a very sharp pair of clean shears. If they aren't sharp they will damage the rose's stem by crushing it. Roses should be cut before 3pm in the afternoon as they need to use the early part of the day to store nutrients. Once a bud is fully opened it is too late to cut. Ideally a rose bud should not be more than open or a half open. To aid in the nourishment of the rose whilst standing in water at least three leaves should be left on the stem. Cut off all leaves on the stem below the water line as these will rot and poison the water. Once the water starts getting cloudy it should be replaced with clean hot water.

Cause of wilting cut roses

When it comes to cutting the stems it is important to remove any air that can enter it as this will reduce the life of the bloom. One way to prevent this from happening is to cut the stem under the water. Another method is to stand them in hot water before cutting.

Getting your roses into hot water

Plunging roses into very hot water before arranging can prolong their life. Hot water has also shown itself invaluable for reviving wilted roses. The causes of wilted roses are many; one is because of bacteria in the water. Hot water has the ability to kill bacteria and give roses a new lease on life.

How to cut roses

One of the reasons roses wilt is because they have lost the moisture within their cell structure. This often happens when roses have been cut too early before being placed in a vase or if they have been left standing out of water for too long. To revive them again it is necessary to re-hydrate these cells so that they can once again deliver water to the foliage.

Wilting cut roses

If you find your roses wilting, take them out of the vase and cut of about 1/8th off of their stems. Place them into hot water and let them stand for about an hour before rearranging them back in a clean vase filled with fresh water.

At times it appears that only one or two blooms wilt when the others are fine. If this is the case it may be due to an air pocket being lodged in the stem. A rose uses its stem to draw water and if this process is impeded by an air lock as a result of cutting, water cannot move up the stem and the bloom will droop.

To remove this airlock is simple. Simply take the dropping or wilted roses out of the vase re-cut their stems and place them into boiling water for about an hour before putting them back into the vase. This simple yet effective cure will ensure that your roses are once again restored back to their full beauty, head held high.

Importance of humidity and air movement in preventing diseases

High relative humidity is one of the major factors contributing to mildew and disease problems in the greenhouse. High humidity is especially troublesome when greenhouses are tightly sealed to conserve energy. Cool nights also increase humidity. Warm air holds more moisture than cold air. During warm days the greenhouse air picks up moisture. As the air cools in the evening, especially during spring and fall, the moisture-holding capacity drops until the dew point is reached and water begins to condense on surfaces.

Relative humidity can be lowered by three methods:

Keep the vents open an inch or so (or run exhaust fans at low capacity) when the heat comes on in the late afternoon. This allows cooler air to enter the greenhouse while warm moist air leaves. As the entering cooler air is heated, relative humidity drops. After 5 to 10 minutes, close vents or turn off fans.

When extremely moist conditions exist in a greenhouse, it may be necessary to exchange the air several times at night. Equipment can be purchased to turn on exhaust fans at predetermined times.The fans should remain on long enough to exhaust one volume of air. Heat loss is small, since the mass of the exhausted air is small relative to the combined mass of the greenhouse structure, plants, media, floor, etc., which hold heat inside the greenhouse. Humidity can further be reduced by watering early in the day when the warm air can absorb moisture from wet surfaces.

Moving air in the closed greenhouse helps reduce water on plant surfaces. A horizontal air flow system or the overhead polyethylene ventilation tube system minimizes temperature differentials and cold spots where condensation is likely to occur. The horizontal air flow (HAF) system is described below.

Overgrown plants are more prone to diseases such as Botrytis and make it difficult to obtain adequate fungicide coverage. Proper planting dates, plant nutrition, watering practices and height management techniques help to prevent lush, overgrown plants. Proper spacing will also lower humidity within the plant canopy.

How to get your rose bloom more

What is the bloom cycle? This is the time it takes the rose bush to produce another flower. The beginning of the cycle is the moment you deadhead off the old bloom and the end is when a new bloom opens up.

Why would we want to do this? Say you have a party coming up in August and you want your roses in full bloom for the event. Or maybe a backyard wedding. Maybe you need a lot of cut flowers for a special event. Or your in-laws are coming to visit and you want to score some points. Regardless of your reasons it's a fun thing to know how to do.

Timing the bloom cycle involves cutting off all blooms and buds so the bloom cycle for the entire bush begins and ends at the same time. Exhibitors do this to get ready for a big show. We'll start with how to do it and then you can use the chart below to determine what the bloom cycle is for your particular plant.

How to begin

You do this via normal deadheading techniques. You count down to the second or third leaflet group and make your cut at an angle just above it. With shrub roses I don't worry much about inward or outward facing eyes. I just make sure I'm cutting above healthy vigorous growth. Now, during normal deadheading we only have to worry about cutting off the blooms that are faded or no longer have petals. This encourages the bush to constantly replenish itself and gives you a pretty constant bloom over the growing year.

But for this we are trying to time the bush to cover itself in blooms all at once. Not only one bush but your whole garden. Beautiful? Yes. But it calls for radical surgery to pull it off. All the blooms, new and old, and all the buds have to be cut off. No exceptions. A true expert can play with this rule but this kind of touch is beyond most of us.

If you are hesitant with this practice, try experimenting first on only one plant to see the results.

How to Transplant Roses

There are several reasons why you might want to transplant your blooming roses. It might be that something is blocking it from getting enough sunlight or you wanted to redesign your garden and you wanted your rose bush to take the center stage. Whatever your reasons may be, it is important to note that transplanting roses require a certain methodology so that their growth will not be hampered. So before you uproot that beautiful rose from its comfortable spot, there are a couple of things that you need to familiarize with before transplanting the roses.

First you must select a suitable area where you are going to plant the roses, then make the necessary preparations on the new spot as well as with the rose that needs to be transplanted. Make sure that the root ball will not be exposed to a very hot condition since it needs to maintain the moisture in its roots. The rose should be prepared by watering it the day before it will be transplanted. Just like any living organism that goes to another place, water is the main key for a successful transplant. If the roots have lots of moisture when they are transplanted, then they would not be compelled to absorb water in a new spot where they have not yet adapted to. So generally, a plant full of water has a greater chance of survival when transplanted compared to a dry and wilted one.

After preparing and knowing everything, the next thing to do is to actually dig out the rose. Do not be afraid to do this, just make sure that you keep the root ball intact and that you do not cut the roots in the process of digging it out.

Hold the crown, and by using a 12-inch spade, burying every single inch of the spade into the ground at the base of the rose, move it carefully around the base to make a circumference, and then carefully pull it out, supporting the root ball all the time.

The hole where you will transfer the rose should be covered in mulch. Newly transplanted plants need moisture and the mulch would come in handy. Remember that the rose should be slightly higher than before so as not to smother the stems. When you see that the plant has started to wilt after transplanting, this means that it is experiencing a hard time to support its top structure. When this happens, all you need to do is add more water. You can also prune the wilted tips.

Always remember the preparations that you should make before transplanting a rose. Do not transplant it during its growing season since the plant may be shocked, the reason why most plant gurus would recommend transplanting a dormant rose.

Caring for Roses in Different Seasons

Caring for roses during different seasons such as spring, summer, fall and winter requires skills, patience and basic knowledge in order for you to maintain a healthy and beautiful bloom throughout the year. As you read through, you will notice how each season prepares you for the next. When each new season arrives, a different type of gardening practices should be observed so that your roses can deal with the different conditions each season brings. Rose care is not just one single step to take, but many that coincide with the changing of the seasons. Here are easy steps you can follow.

Spring

Caring for roses at springtime is one of the happiest

tasks for rose gardeners because it signals the start of a new growing season. You look forward to getting out in your garden and enjoy the warm spring sunshine. This is also when you expect the rosebuds to appear. Since your roses may have been covered with dirt during winter, here are the steps you should follow:

- Gently remove the dirt (or protective covering) so that your rose plants can experience warmth of the spring sunshine or occasional spring rain.

- Before pruning, remove winter mulch, dead canes, debris, and fallen leaves and clean the surroundings thoroughly.

- Add organic compounds to the soil for nutrients.

- Make sure soil is well-drained with not stagnant water under the bushes.

- Spring is also a time to ready your roses for the summer heat and diseases. Spray or soak your roses with a non-toxic treatment like baking soda solution.

Summer

When caring for your rose bushes during summer,

provide deep watering for your roses to keep them hydrated throughout the hot, dry season. Soak them with water once a week if you are living in a moderate climate. For hotter regions, water your roses more than usual. Target the roots when you are watering, not the leaves.

It is also important to continue with your fertilizing, disease-prevention and watering regimen. This will keep your rose healthy and ready for cutting the blooms and making bou quets. Fertilize your roses every 3-4 weeks or after flower growth.

Make sure you consult with experts the type of pesticide or herbicide for the right disease.

Autumn

Rose care during autumn is preparation for winter and continuing what you did in the summer.

Consider preparing the following for your rose beds for the winter:

- Spraying. Continue regular spray

- Clean-up. Try to keep the ground or mulch in your rose beds free from weeds and rose litter.

Winter

Caring for your roses during winter is different. Allow your roses to harden in the freezing temperature for about two weeks to prevent new growth. Mound 8- 12 inches of winter mulch over the crown and cover with burlap as protection to the exposed parts. Spray with oils and fungicides to kill any diseases that might develop over the winter.

When you are caring for roses in your garden, learn the seasonal way of caring for them, because whatever the season is, you will be able to anticipate a healthy bloom and enjoy beautiful flowers your rose garden would bring.

Common pest and diseases

Rose Disease - Treatment and Prevention

Rose diseases and pest are something every gardener encounters and can range from problematic to devastating for your garden plants. By following basic preventive steps you can protect your garden from disease and pests. There are few common diseases to watch for which can easily be identified and kept in check.

Powdery Mildew

If rose leaves begin to drop and look white and powdery they may have Powdery Mildew. It is a fungus which is found on the underside of leaves. The best prevention is to control moisture on plant foliage by watering plants directly at the base of the plant, on the soil. To rid your plant of mildew organically, mix one teaspoon of baking soda with a half teaspoon of cooking oil and add to a quart of warm water. Take the mixture and spray it on the affected leaves. Should leaves drop, be sure to dispose of them outside of the garden so as not to spread the fungus.

Rust

Another common disease caused by too much moisture is Rust, the orange powder found on foliage, usually on the underside of the leaf. Remove diseased leaves immediately to control spreading. If necessary a chemical treatment can be used for the rose.

Blackspot

Small black spots, about ½" round are signs of the fungal disease - aptly named - Blackspot. This is one of the more devastating fungi, as it will kill roses if left untreated. When the spots appear, remove the damaged parts of the flower; if it continues try a fungicide.

Rose Mosaic

Most rose diseases are of the fungus variety, the exception is rose mosaic which is a virus. It looks like a mosaic of green or yellow spots on the plant's leaves. Removing and destroying the leaves is the only effective treatment.

Canker

Dark red or brown spots, or indentations on plant canes, are from Canker. It enters and infects roses through cuts or wounds and can be difficult to kill. Cut the diseased canes off to stop the progress of this disease.

Rose Disease Prevention

There are some basic steps gardeners can take to help prevent the spread of rose diseases:

- Keep moisture away from plant leaves by always watering directly in the soil at the base of the plant.

- Stick to a regular schedule of fertilizing roses; healthy plants are more immune to pests and disease.

- In addition to deadheading and pruning, remember to seal cuts immediately with white glue.

- Use clean pruners, rubbed with alcohol after each cutting. Do not allow disease to spread through tools.

- Clear the garden beds of debris and leaves on a regular basis, throw all foliage and plant cuttings in a garbage can, away from the garden.

Following these basic precautions will help control rose disease, improve the health of your roses and provide an environment where plants can flourish.

How to get rid of Japanese beetles

Good horticultural practices, including watering and fertilizing, will reduce the damage caused by these beetles, but oftentimes you simply need to get rid of them. Here are some ideas:

Row Covers: Protect your plants from Japanese beetles with row covers during the 6- to 8-week feeding period.

Hand Pick: Unfortunately, one of the most effective way of getting rid of Japanese beetles, without using chemicals, is to hand pick them. It's time consuming, but it works, especially if you are diligent. When you pick them off, put them in a solution of 1 tablespoon of liquid dishwashing detergent and water, which will cause them to drown.

Neem oil: Neem oil and sprays containing potassium bicarbonate are somewhat effective, especially on roses. The adults ingest a chemical in the neem oil and pass it on in their eggs, and the resulting larvae die before they become adults. Note that Neem can be harmful to fish and should be reapplied after rainstorms.

Use a Dropcloth: Put down a dropcloth and, in the early morning when they're most active, shake them off and dump them into a bucket of soapy water. They will not survive.

Insecticides: If you wish to spray or dust with insecticides, speak to your local cooperative or garden center about approved insecticides in your area.

Or, try this safe homemade solution: Mix 1 teaspoon of liquid dishwashing detergent with 1 cup of vegetable oil and shake well; then add it to 1 quart of water. Add 1 cup of rubbing alcohol and shake vigorously to emulsify. Pour this mixture into a spray bottle and use it at ten-day intervals on pests. Homemade sprays can run more of a risk of damaging plant leaves, so be careful.

Apply sprays in the morning, never in full sun or at temperatures above 90°F. If your plants start to wilt, rinse the leaves immediately with clean water.

Traps: Japanese beetle traps can be helpful in controlling large numbers of beetles, but they also might attract beetles from beyond your yard.

Eugenol and geraniol, aromatic chemicals extracted from plants, are attractive to adult Japanese beetles as well as to other insects. Unfortunately, the traps do not effectively suppress adults and might even result in a higher localized population. If you want to try them, be sure to place traps far away from plants so that the beetles do not land on your favored plants on their way to the traps.

Fruit Cocktail: You can buy Japanese beetle traps of all sorts, but most are no more effective than a can of fruit cocktail. Open the can and let it sit in the sun for a week to ferment. Then place it on top of bricks or wood blocks in a light-colored pail, and fill the pail with water to just below the top of the can. Place the pail about 25 feet from the plants you want to protect. The beetles will head for the sweet bait, fall into the water, and drown. If rain dilutes the bait, start over.

Geraniums: Japanese beetles are attracted to geraniums. They eat the blossoms, promptly get dizzy, fall down, and permit you to dispose of them conveniently with a dustpan and brush. Plant geraniums close to more valuable plants which you wish to save from the ravages of Japanese beetles.

Japanese beetles on Roses? Note that insecticides will not fully protect roses, which unfold too fast and are especially attractive to beetles. When beetles are most abundant on roses, nip the buds and spray the bushes to protect the leaves. When the beetles become scarce, let the bushes bloom again. Timeliness and thoroughness of application are very important. Begin treatment as soon as beetles appear, before damage is done.

NOTE: Many dusts or sprays are highly toxic to honeybees. If application of these materials to plants is necessary during the bloom period, do not apply during hours when bees are visiting the flowers. If larger than yard and garden plantings are to be treated, you may need to contact nearby beekeepers in advance so that they can protect their colonies.

Special Thanks

Thank you for reading! Hopefully you found this information to be incredibly helpful in achieving a thriving rose garden. If you would like to show your appreciation, a simple review on amazon would be very helpful. Thank and happy rose gardening!

Printed in Great Britain
by Amazon